NED KELLY
and the odd rellie

50 micro lives of the great Australians

Gerard Windsor | *illustrated by Michel Streich*

First published 2007 by University of Queensland Press
PO Box 6042, St Lucia, Queensland 4067 Australia

www.uqp.uq.edu.au

© 2007 Gerard Windsor and Michel Streich

Printed in China by Everbest
Book design by Michel Streich, Sydney

Cataloguing in Publication Data
National Library of Australia

Windsor, Gerard, 1944–.
Ned Kelly and the odd rellie.
ISBN 0 7022 3578 4.
I. Streich, Michel. II. Title.
A823.3

1 | James Cook
Gave New Zealand a look.
'Ah, I'll give you a hoy
When I discover Bondoi.'

2 | Arthur Phillip
Longed to trill, 'Hip
Hip Hooray!'
On Australia Day.

3 | Bennelong
Was done wrong –
His house on the Point
For the rest of the joint.

4 | William Bligh
Cried, 'Fee Fi
Fo Fum'
Whenever he got a whiff of rum.

5 | Liz Macarthur
Saw weeds on the path. 'Ah,
I'll need,' she said, 'to keep
A sheep.'

6 | Matthew Flinders
Felt his world turn to cinders
When George Bass yelled, 'Scat!'
At Trim, his cat.

7 | Mrs Macquarie
Said, 'I'm not at all sorry
That spot is so bare.
You can put my chair there.'

8 | Caroline Chisholm
Clutched girls to her b'som.
'Never accept sweets
And keep off the streets.'

9 | Ned Kelly
And the odd rellie
Thought it a real hoot
To slip on a boiler suit.

Mary MacKillop
Needed a fillip.
The Devil might hiss 'n all;
Her brandy was just medicinal.

Banjo Paterson
Was torn by the critics to tatters an'
Then cheered by the sporty set
For a good thing out of Old Regret.

12 | Ethel Turner
Said, 'I'll put it on the backburner.
I can't see how the tale ends
For six little Australians.'

13 | Mrs Aeneas Gunn
Thought the family name overdone.
'It's just Jack, Jeannie, Kev, er…
You know, us of the Never Never.'

14 | Tom Roberts
Cried, 'It' (sob) 'hurts,
But Arthur Streeton
Has me beaten.'

15 | Henry Lawson
Was not Douglas Mawson.
'On the rocks' was his vice.
Doug liked ice.

Les Darcy
Was world classy.
So the Yanks fixed our national treasure,
And Phar Lap too for good measure.

17 | May Gibbs
Couldn't abide fibs.
Any nut with that yen
Was fed to the banksia men.

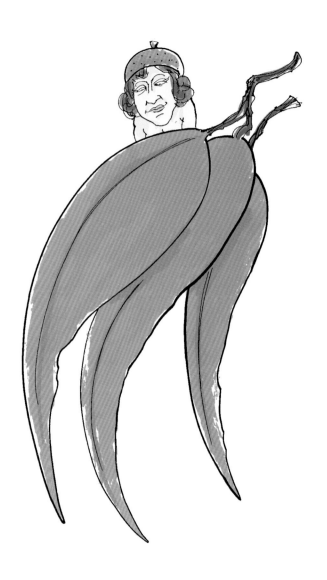

18 | Billy Hughes
Held strident views
When he came to speak
For his party of the week.

John Monash
Had fans en masse.
Unlike Tom Blamey
Who hadn't one *ami*.

20 | Nellie Melba
Gave a touch of her elber
To any impresario
Who said no to another go.

Howard Florey
Found penicillin, or he
Thought he had till Alexander Fleming
Started aheming.

Errol Flynn
Winked, 'I've got an in
To any desirable lane
On the Spanish Main.'

23 | John Curtin
Knew the Poms weren't certain.
'Well, I'll take a Yank this Fall
To the Coral Sea Ball.'

Ben Chifley,
All too briefly,
Drove the train
On the Monaro plain.

D. G. Bradman
Transferred to Admin
When a quick duck
Showed he was out of luck.

26 | Bea Miles
Was all smiles
When the cabbie took her to Sumatra
For three acts of *Ant and Cleopatra*.

27 | Sir Robert Gordon Menzies
Sent the workers into frenzies.
Though he acted such a nob
He was only Pig-Iron Bob.

28 | Marjorie Jackson
Missed the facts on
A baton grip
That didn't slip.

29 | Johnny O'Keefe
Found it a relief
To get off his rocks
Around the clocks.

Dawn Fraser
Felt it wouldn't faze her
To nick a flag
To wrap the gold she had in the bag.

Albert Namatjira
Was no one's inferior.
Dots gave others thrills.
He just liked hills.

32 | Patrick White
Bred dogs with no bite,
Extracting their barks
For use in his own remarks.

33 | Evonne Goolagong
Kidded many a fool along.
They said, 'She's gone walkabout'
When she fancied hitting a ball out.

Harry Seidler
Was no idler.
He'd give you a tall box faster
Than you could say 'Disaster'.

35 | Gough Whitlam
Ran a hit jam
Session till John Kerr
Stopped his enc're.

36 | Malcolm Fraser
Was fond of a blazer,
But thought trousers
An affectation of wowsers.

37 | Bob Hawke
Was no dork.
Life was all piss
And kiss.

Brett Whiteley
Found Wendy very sightly.
Everything *plein air*
Had her derrière.

39 | Joan Sutherland
Sang, 'On the other hand
The sight of Bonynge
Fills the voice with longing.'

40 | Barry Humphries
Promised, 'No words like bum. Please,
My Edna's not shady,
She's a true Australian lady.'

41 | Germaine Greer
Gave a flea in the ear
To most of the human noise,
But she excepted boys.

Jenny Kee
Grinned with glee.
'Life won't get duller,
I've found a new colour!'

43 | Paul Keating
Doubted porkies were cheating.
John Howard
Held they were always allowed.

44 | Rene Rivkin
Was rather a spiv. Can
Large rocks, young men and cigars
Lead anywhere but behind bars?

45 | Kerry Packer
Pocketed a stack o'
Chips. 'What the fuck
Can I do with this muck?'

46 | Collette Dinnigan
Had to begin again
Whenever her stuff
Wasn't flimsy enough.

47 | Dr Peter Jensen
Thought it impolite to mention
That papist George Pell
Was en route to Hell.

48 | Kylie Minogue
Was always in vogue.
Neighbours was creaky,
But wasn't she cheeky!

49 | Russell Crowe
Growled, 'I'm all muscle so
Mention phone scandals
You'll feel a sword and sandals'.

Shane Warne
Could have sworn
It was just the one blonde
Of whom he was fond.

Biographies

1| JAMES COOK (1728–1779) circumnavigated and charted New Zealand in 1769 and, the following year, landed on and mapped much of the eastern coast of Australia.

2| ARTHUR PHILLIP (1738–1814), the first governor of New South Wales, raised the British flag in Sydney Cove on 26 January 1788.

3| BENNELONG (1764?–1813), a member of the Wangal people, had a brick house built for him in 1791 on the eastern arm of Sydney Cove now known as Bennelong Point. The Sydney Opera House stands there today.

4| WILLIAM BLIGH (1754–1817), fourth governor of NSW, tried unsuccessfully to curb the colony's rum economy.

5| ELIZABETH MACARTHUR (1767?–1803) and her husband JOHN (1767–1834) are seen as the founders of the Australian wool industry.

6| MATTHEW FLINDERS (1774–1814) and GEORGE BASS (1771–1803) made several exploratory voyages together along the Australian coasts. A statue of Flinders' cat, TRIM, stands near that of his master outside the State Library of New South Wales.

7| ELIZABETH MACQUARIE (1778–1835), wife of the fifth governor of NSW, was keenly interested in gardening, landscaping and agriculture. The spit of open crown land immediately to the east of Bennelong Point on Sydney Harbour is known as Mrs Macquarie's Chair.

8| CAROLINE CHISHOLM (1808–1877) worked tirelessly for the assisted migration of young women and families to Australia and, once arrived, their employment and placement on land holdings.

9| NED KELLY (1855–1880), the leader of Australia's most famous gang of bushrangers, was captured wearing his homemade armour.

10| MARY MACKILLOP (1842–1909) founded the Josephite nuns to teach poor children. The process of her canonisation was troubled by rumours of a taste for drink.

11| BANJO PATERSON (1864–1941), Australia's most popular balladeer, wrote *The Man from Snowy River* in 1890.

12| ETHEL TURNER (1870–1958) wrote numerous books for young adults, the first and best-known being *Seven Little Australians*, published in 1894.

13| JEANNIE GUNN (1870–1961) wrote *We of the Never Never*, an account of her married life on Elsey Station in the Northern Territory. Her husband AENEAS died after they had been there just a year.

14| TOM ROBERTS (1856–1931) and ARTHUR STREETON (1867–1943) were the leading lights of the group of artists known as the Heidelberg School.

15| HENRY LAWSON (1867–1922), the great short story chronicler of rural Australia, became a hopeless alcoholic. DOUGLAS MAWSON (1882–1958) was a scientist and Antarctic explorer.

16| LES DARCY (1895–1917), a hero of the Australian boxing world, died of pneumonia while on a tour of the United States. PHAR LAP (1926–1932), a racehorse, died in the US of internal bleeding, possibly poisoning, while on his way to race America's best.

17| MAY GIBBS (1877–1969) wrote and illustrated *Snugglepot and Cuddlepie* and other stories of the gumnut babies and their flora and fauna world.

18| BILLY HUGHES (1862–1952), prime minister from 1915 to 1922, began his career as a Labor politician but went on to represent most political parties in the Australian parliament.

19| JOHN MONASH (1865–1931) was the greatly admired commander of the Australian troops during the First World War. THOMAS BLAMEY (1884–1951) was their much disliked commander in the Second.

20| NELLIE MELBA (1861–1931), Australia's first international prima donna and artistic celebrity, regularly made 'positively last appearances'.

21| HOWARD FLOREY (1895–1968) pioneered the therapeutic use of penicillin, a substance first isolated in 1928 by ALEXANDER FLEMING.

22| ERROL FLYNN (1909–1959) made the swashbuckling movie his specialty, and had a colourful sexual reputation.

23| JOHN CURTIN (1885–1945), prime minister from 1941 to 1945, accepted that Australia's security lay with the United States. For many years the significant naval victory of May 1942 was commemorated by Coral Sea Week and its ball.

24| BEN CHIFLEY (1885–1951), a former train driver, was prime minister from 1945 to 1949.

25| DONALD BRADMAN (1908–2001) was bowled second ball in his last test innings. He later spent many years as chairman of the Australian Cricket Board of Control and as a selector.

26| BEA MILES (1902–1973), Australia's most famous bag lady, wore a placard advertising readings from Shakespeare for a shilling or sixpence. She was also a persistent hijacker of taxis.

27| ROBERT MENZIES (1894–1978), Liberal prime minister from 1939 to 1941 and from 1949 to 1966, had a deep sentimental attachment to the British monarchical system.

28| MARJORIE JACKSON (1931–), known as 'the Lithgow Flash', won the 100m and 200m sprints at the 1952 Helsinki Olympic Games. Australia was leading on the last leg of the 4 x 100m relay when the baton fell or was dislodged from her hand.

29| JOHNNY O'KEEFE (1935–1978), Australia's king of rock 'n' roll, compered ABC TV's Saturday night show, *Six O'Clock Rock*.

30| DAWN FRASER (1937–) won the 100m freestyle at three consecutive Olympic Games. At the last, in Tokyo in 1964, she souvenired a Japanese flag and was subsequently banned from competitive swimming for ten years.

31| ALBERT NAMATJIRA (1902–1959), member of the Arrernte people, became known in the 1950s for his watercolour landscapes, but was later neglected in favour of the apparently more traditional dot painting style developed at Papunya.

32| PATRICK WHITE (1912–1990), the Nobel Prize-winning novelist, bred schnauzers for some years. He had a caustic tongue.

33| EVONNE GOOLAGONG (1951–), a member of the Wiradjuri people, won seven grand slam singles titles including Wimbledon in 1971 and 1980. Her Aboriginal heritage was sometimes invoked to explain her playing style.

34| HARRY SEIDLER (1923–2006) was Australia's most significant modernist architect.

35| GOUGH WHITLAM (1916–), prime minister from 1972 to 1975, led a liberating, innovative but somewhat anarchic Labor government. He was controversially dismissed by the Governor-General SIR JOHN KERR (1914–1991).

36| MALCOLM FRASER (1930–), prime minister from 1975 to 1983, was of a patrician background and bearing. In 1986, in Memphis, Tennessee, he appeared trouserless in a hotel lobby.

37| BOB HAWKE (1929–), prime minister from 1983 to 1991, was renowned as both a fast and frequent consumer of alcohol and as a ladies' man.

38| BRETT WHITELEY (1939–1992) featured his wife, WENDY, or parts of her, in many of his paintings.

39| JOAN SUTHERLAND (1926–), one of the world's great sopranos, enjoyed a mutually fruitful partnership with her husband, the conductor RICHARD BONYNGE (1930–).

40| BARRY HUMPHRIES (1934–), writer and actor, is best known for his creation of Edna Everage, the superstar housewife from Moonee Ponds.

41| GERMAINE GREER (1939–), Australia's greatest feminist and gadfly. In 2003 she published *The Beautiful Boy*, a paean to teenage males.

42| JENNY KEE (1947–) came to prominence in the 1970s as a fashion designer of shimmering bright clothes.

43| PAUL KEATING (1944–), prime minister from 1991 to 1996, was accused of unsavoury dealings in a piggery he owned. JOHN HOWARD (1939–), prime minister since 1996, is widely regarded as being economical with the truth.

44| RENE RIVKIN (1944–2005), flamboyant stockbroker and Sydney identity, was convicted of insider trading and eventually served periodic detention.

45| KERRY PACKER (1937–2005), tycoon and gambler.

46| COLLETTE DINNIGAN (1966–), fashion designer with a preference for a minimalist style.

47| PETER JENSEN (1943–), evangelical Anglican archbishop of Sydney, but having curiously much in common with GEORGE CARDINAL PELL (1941–), Catholic archbishop of Sydney.

48| KYLIE MINOGUE (1968–), actor and pop star with an oft-reinvented and strikingly durable career.

49| RUSSELL CROWE (1964–), actor and macho identity, known for his role in *Gladiator* and for throwing a phone at a New York hotel receptionist.

50| SHANE WARNE (1969–) leg-spinner and devotee of people with golden hair.

THE AUTHOR

GERARD WINDSOR's diverse publications include novels, short stories, essays, and memoirs. His ninth and most recent book was the novel *I Have Kissed Your Lips*, and in 2005 he was awarded the Pascall Prize for Criticism.

THE ILLUSTRATOR

MICHEL STREICH was born in Westphalia, Germany. After starting his artistic career there, he worked as an illustrator in London for several years, finally basing himself in Sydney in 2000. Michel has contributed drawings to a wide variety of magazines and newspapers, among them *The Bulletin*, *The Sydney Morning Herald*, the *Australian Financial Review*, *The Sun-Herald*, *Australian Gourmet Traveller*, as well as *The Times* and the *Financial Times*.